The Turnage Family Genealogy

Introduction

This book is about the Turnage Family History. My grandmother was Ivie Turnage who married Harold Clarence Fletcher. Discovering our own family history is so important for so many reasons. It gives us a sense of where we came from and who we are. It reminds us how strong our ancestors were and how we can be strong and brave too. We are the pieces of all who came before us.

Our ancestors lived remarkable lives and were brave enough to leave their homelands in foreign countries and come to America to start over. They settled this country, raised families, went through wars, disease and constant change. They were remarkable people in a new land called America and paved the way for many of the things we hold dear – constitutional rights, freedom of religion and speech, education, morals, values, attitudes and belief systems. We inherited all of these from our various ancestors.

We are also a true mix of many different races, cultures and religions. Our ancestors did come from foreign countries all over the world. Once they got to America they married people from different backgrounds, races. They intermixed with the Native Indians, had children with their slaves and intertwined many different races, cultures. America is truly a "melting pot".

Dedication

This book is dedicated to all my family members and my Grandmother Ivie Turnage Fletcher. Also to all my descendants.

THE TURNAGE NOTES / HISTORY / LOCATIONS

LOCATIONS WHERE TURNAGES LIVED

Tipton, TN – 1814 to present
Hardin Co, TN
Smith, TN – 1800-1850
Crittenden, AK
Chesterfield, SC – 1785 -1870
Pitt, NC (around Greenville, NC) – 1747-1800
Bertie, NC (around Greenville, NC) 1700-1770
Essex England (close to London) 1647 and before

* Pitt Co, NC is considered the ancestral home of the American Turnage families

Also linked to Turnages in Cripple Creek, CO

TURNAGES STILL LIVE IN

Tipton, Henderson Co Tennessee, Pitt Co, NC, some in New Bern, NC,

TURNAGE IS AN ENGLISH NAME

George Turnage Jr was the founding father of our American Turnage families. They are from Great Waltham, Essex England. Our ancestors in Essex County, England apparently took their name from just such a site where Thunor was worshipped. It means literally "a place where Thunor is worshipped".

Thor was the god of thunder and the chief god of farmers.

LAND OWNERS

Most were farmers, some owned more acreage than others. In 1777 William bought 200 acres from his grandfather George (1738)

In 1778 Jacob Blount gave Isaac Turnage several slaves

Isaac Turnage owned 14 slaves in 1860 in Tipton, TN and so did some of his brothers and relatives

HOW MANY ARE THERE?

There are over 50,000 kinfolk in the world with the Turnage lineage. 115 Turnages fought on the Confederate side of the Civil war. Eight Turnages fought on the Union Side.

MY TURNAGE FAMILY

My Turnage Family came from Essex, England and moved to Bertie, NC, then to Pitt Co, NC, on to Chesterfield, SC and eventually Tipton, TN.

Generation One:
The author – Katherine Fletcher

Generation Two
Hayes Fletcher (1932-) and Margaret Anita Rice

Generation Three
Ivie Myrtle Turnage (1904-1998) and Harold Fletcher (1904-1983)

Generation Four:
John Alta Turnage (1867-1959) and Mittie George (1874-1942)

Generation Five:
Isaac Newton Turnage (1841-1882) and Ellen Hunt

Generation Six:
Isaac William Turnage (1799-1870) and Purity Gibson

Generation Seven:
William Turnage (1774-1827) and Elizabeth ____(had many wives)

Generation Eight:
William Turnage (1747-1823) and Mary ___ and other wives

Generation Nine:
Luke Turnage (1731-1818) and Rachel ____?

Generation Ten:
William George Turnage (1700-1736) and Sarah (Selah) Needham

Generation Eleven: Essex, England to USA
George Turnage (1671-after 1736) and Elizabeth White

Generation Twelve:
George Turnage (1647-1672) and Mary _____?

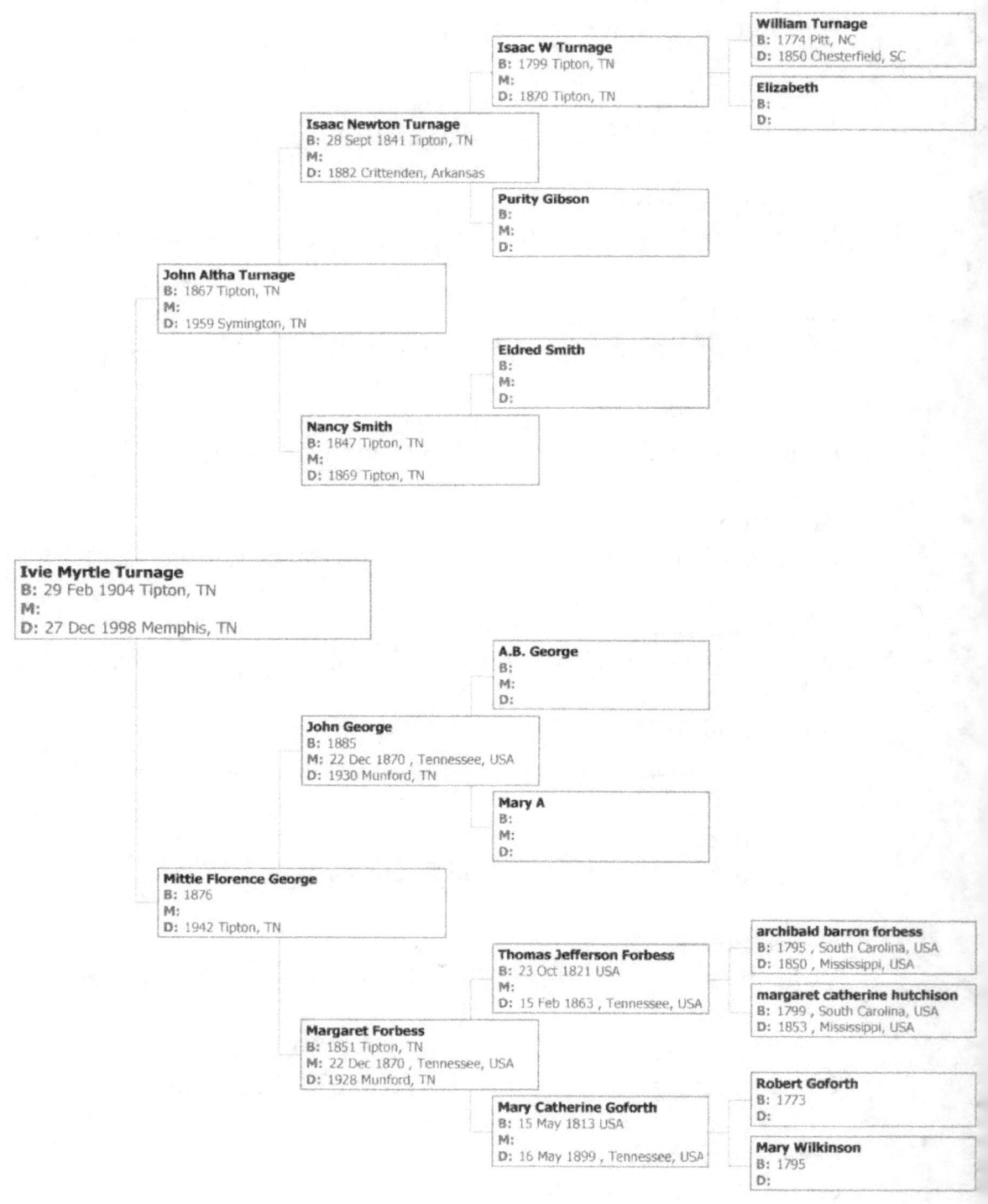

Isaac W Turnage
B: 1799 Tipton, TN
M:
D: 1870 Tipton, TN

William Turnage
B: 1774 Pitt, NC
D: 1850 Chesterfield, SC

Elizabeth
B:
D:

Isaac Newton Turnage
B: 28 Sept 1841 Tipton, TN
M:
D: 1882 Crittenden, Arkansas

Purity Gibson
B:
M:
D:

John Altha Turnage
B: 1867 Tipton, TN
M:
D: 1959 Symington, TN

Eldred Smith
B:
M:
D:

Nancy Smith
B: 1847 Tipton, TN
M:
D: 1869 Tipton, TN

Ivie Myrtle Turnage
B: 29 Feb 1904 Tipton, TN
M:
D: 27 Dec 1998 Memphis, TN

A.B. George
B:
M:
D:

John George
B: 1885
M: 22 Dec 1870 , Tennessee, USA
D: 1930 Munford, TN

Mary A
B:
M:
D:

Mittie Florence George
B: 1876
M:
D: 1942 Tipton, TN

Thomas Jefferson Forbess
B: 23 Oct 1821 USA
M:
D: 15 Feb 1863 , Tennessee, USA

archibald barron forbess
B: 1795 , South Carolina, USA
D: 1850 , Mississippi, USA

margaret catherine hutchison
B: 1799 , South Carolina, USA
D: 1853 , Mississippi, USA

Margaret Forbess
B: 1851 Tipton, TN
M: 22 Dec 1870 , Tennessee, USA
D: 1928 Munford, TN

Mary Catherine Goforth
B: 15 May 1813 USA
M:
D: 16 May 1899 , Tennessee, USA

Robert Goforth
B: 1773
D:

Mary Wilkinson
B: 1795
D:

6

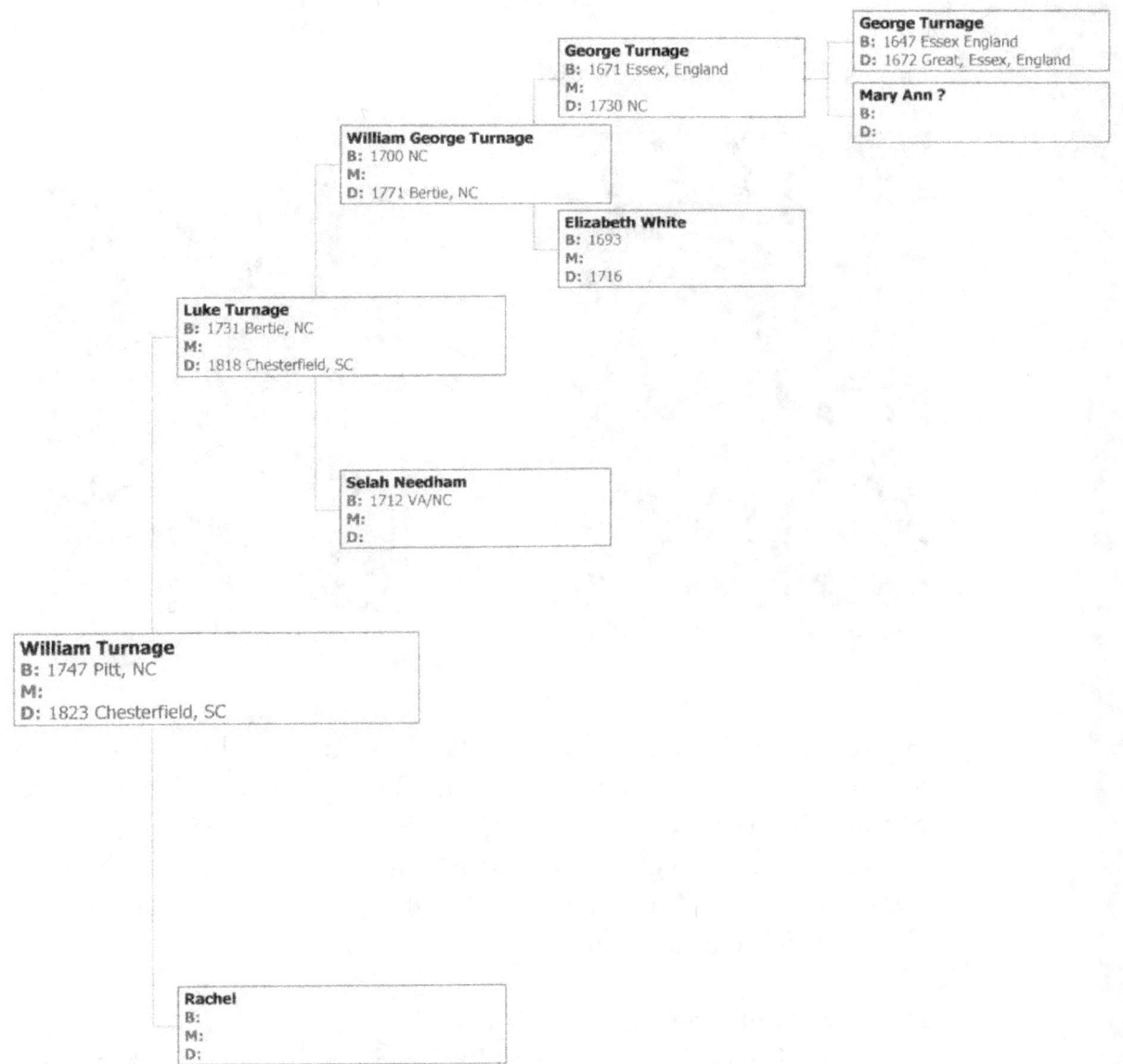

George Turnage
B: 1671 Essex, England
M:
D: 1730 NC

George Turnage
B: 1647 Essex England
D: 1672 Great, Essex, England

Mary Ann ?
B:
D:

William George Turnage
B: 1700 NC
M:
D: 1771 Bertie, NC

Elizabeth White
B: 1693
M:
D: 1716

Luke Turnage
B: 1731 Bertie, NC
M:
D: 1818 Chesterfield, SC

Selah Needham
B: 1712 VA/NC
M:
D:

William Turnage
B: 1747 Pitt, NC
M:
D: 1823 Chesterfield, SC

Rachel
B:
M:
D:

GENERATION TWO:

Hayes Fletcher and Anita Rice

Hayes and Anita Fletcher

Hayes Fletcher

Hayes Fentress Fletcher, son of Harold Clarence Fletcher and Ivie Myrtle Turnage was born in 1932 in Covington, TN. He grew up in Memphis, Adamsville, Atwood, and Paducah, Ky. with his five brothers and one sister. He graduated from Lambuth College in Jackson, TN. in 1954 and received his Master of Divinity degree from Garrett Theological Seminary in Evanston, Ill in 1958.

He served churches in the following communities in Northern Illinois (Chicago Area): Arlington Heights, Mundelein, Belvidere, and Oak Park. He was active in the Civil Rights movement and the anti-Vietnam War movement during the sixties. He left the pastoral ministry in 1971 and moved his family to Connecticut, where he worked in New York and Stamford, CT. The family moved to Jackson, TN in 1976, where he served on the administrative staff of Lambuth College for ten years, the last four as Vice President for Development. For five years, he wrote a weekly newspaper column for the Jackson Sun.

In 1988, he became President of Methodist Hospitals Foundation in Memphis, TN. He retired in 1996 and moved with Anita to Weaverville, NC in 2003. After retirement, he wrote and published a book, **Moonbeams from a Jar**, based on his childhood experiences in West Tennessee. He enjoys fishing, golfing and traveling. He is currently working on his autobiography.

GENERATION THREE
Ivie Myrtle Turnage and Harold Clarence Fletcher

Harold Fletcher & Ivie Turnage Fletcher

Harold is my grandfather and lived mostly in Memphis all his life. He was a Methodist Minister. He was born in 1904 and died in 1983.

Ivie M. Turnage was born 2-29-1904 in Tipton, TN. She died in Memphis, TN on 12-27-1998. Her parents were John Altha Turnage and Mittie Florence George from Tipton, TN. She is buried in Helen Crigger Cemetary in Munford, TN.

Harold Fletcher & Ivie Turnage Children:

Jeanna Sue Fletcher
born 5-25-1926,   married: James Russell Coats in 1946,
died 2-27-2003
Children: Ronnie and Sharon

James Norrice Fletcher
Born 6-18-1928 in Tipton, TN;   married Georgia Lamb in 1951
Children: Christie, Vicki, Julie, Amy

Charles Winston Fletcher
Born 2-2-1930 Munford, TN married Jeanne Kirtland 1951
Died: 2009 - Largo, FL
Children: Paul and stepson Charles

Hercel Coy Fletcher
Born: 5-28-1927; Married Beatrice Dunn in 1944
Resides in MS,
Children: Brenda and Dianne

Hayes Fletcher
Born: 10-21-1932 in Covington, TN, married Margaret Anita
Rice 8-4-56
Children: Marc, Suzanne, Katherine, Grant

George Bainbridge Fletcher
Born 6-26-1937, married Jean Holcomb & Donna Faye Wheeler
Children: Michael

Thomas Garry Fletcher
Born 12-30-1944 married Judy Mosier, Chris ?

Hollis Fletcher
Born 4-2-1931 and Died 12-24-1932 (baby)

Coy, Norrice, Thomas, Hayes Fletcher – The Fletcher brothers

GENERATION FOUR
John Altha Turnage and Mittie Florence George

John Altha was born around 1865-1867 in Tipton, TN and died in 1959 in Symington, TN.   His parents are Isaac Newton Turnage and Nancy Smith. He married Mittie George in 1890 in Tipton, TN. They owned a large farm in Burlison, TN.

Mittie Florence George was born 1874-1876 and died in 1942 in Tipton, TN. Her parents were John George (1885-1930) and Margaret Forbess (1851-1928).
Mittie's siblings were Onvie, Acie, Fannie, Allie, Annie, Lillie.

Margaret Forbess's parents were Thomas J. Forbess 1821-1863 and Mary Catherine Goforth (1813-1899). Margaret Forbess siblings are John, Sal, Jim, Tom, Ann and Mary.

Children of John Altha Turnage and Mittie Florence George

Bernice Turnage

Cloudy

Lottie Turnage 1902- married Orville Hayden

Benjamin Marvin Turnage 1892 – 1950 \ married Berta Belle Draffin
  Children: Marvin Lavell Turnage,

Mary (Madie) Agnes Turnage 1894 -

Annie Pearl Turnage 1897 – 1975 married James McClerkin (Calvin)
  Had children: James, Helen Pearl, Billy Joe McClerkin

Elsie M. 1909- married Milton C Glydewell

Gracie Turnage 1899-1987 – married Sherod Bowers

Ivie Myrtle Turnage 1904 - 1998 married Harold C. Fletcher

Earldon Russell Turnage 1914 –1984

Lydia Turnage – 1900 –

Mittie Florence George and John Altha Turnage

Madie, Pearl, Gracie, Lottie, Ivie, Elsie, Earldon, John Altha Turnage
(their father) and Aunt Julia. Taken in 1956.

GENERATION FIVE
Isaac Newton Turnage and Nancy Smith

Isaac Newton Turnage was born 09-28-1841 in Tipton, TN. He died in 1882 in Crittenden, AK. He was married to Nancy Smith and then to Ellen Hunt in 1869. His parents are Isaac W. Turnage and Purity Gibson.

Nancy Smith was born 1847 in Tipton, TN and died there in 1869. Her father was Eldred Smith. Ellen Hunt was born 1848 and died in 1931 in Memphis. Ellen Hunt had a brother named Budd.

Isaac Newton Turnage and Nancy Smith Children:

John Altha Turnage (1867-1959) married Mittie George
    Children: see previous page

Wayne Marshall Turnage – 1869-1941 married Ella May Thompson

Isaac Newton Turnage and Ellen C. Hunt Children:

Edgar Clinton Turnage 1871-1943 married Millie Leona Joyner and then
        Thursy Jones. Children: Ira Lofton, Oscar Calvin, Isaac
Washington (Ike), Stoney Clinton, Albert Sidney, Claude, William

Oliver Anderson Turnage 1875-1942 married Nora Pearl Gross
        Children: Walter F. Ovie E, Gladys I, Solon D
Oliee b 1880 Tipton, TN
Julia Turnage 1877-1966 married Lewis Smith

GENERATION SIX
Isaac William Turnage and Purity Gibson

Isaac W. was born 1799 and died 1870 in Tipton, TN.   He was a farmer. His parents were William Turnage and Elizabeth ? Turnage.
He married Martha Bell in 1819 in Wilson Co, TN. They had five children and she died in 1835. He then married Purity Gibson (1815-1868) in 1835. They had seven more children. They moved to Arkansas before the Civil War.

Children of Isaac W. and Martha Bell married in 1819

Mary Amanda Turnage 1829 Wilson, TN -married A. G. Laxton
Sally – born 1827 Wilson TN
Elizabeth W. 1823 – Wilson, TN
Eliza B. 1820 Wilson, TN
John B. 1825 Wilson, TN
William George 1832 Wilson, TN

Children of Isaac W. and Purity Gibson married 1835:

Isaac Newton Turnage - 1841
 Julie Caroline – born 1837 Tipton, Tn to 1863
Massarah Massey Turnage – 1839 Tipton, TN to 1840 (died 1 year old)
Sarah P. Turnage = 1853-1882 Tipton, Tn; married Rev. Solomon Roan Forbes
Nancy wade Turnage – 1844 Tipton to 1909

GENERATION SEVEN

William Turnage and Elizabeth Turnage / May McLattan / Lavinia Thompson

William was born in 1774 in Pitt, NC and died in 1850 in Chesterfield, SC.

His parents were William Turnage who had 7 wives. William died of Palsy (paralysis or uncontrolled muscle movements) at age 70. He was a farmer and also a slave owner. William's first wife was Elizabeth Turnage, who was born around 1790 and died in 1827. William's second wife was Mary Polly McLattan and his third wife was Lavania Thompson.

William & Elizabeth's children:

Joseph D Turnage b. c 1816 Chesterfield Co, SC
David Turnage b. Aug 1823, d. a 1870
James P Turnage b. 13 Dec 1826, d. c 1862
Isaac Turnage 1799 SC to 1870 Tipton, TN
James Turnage 1795 -

William's second wife was Mary Polly McLattan. They married in 1815.

William's third wife was Lavinia Thompson. They married in 1827. Lavinia died in Chesterfield, SC. Lavinia Thompson b. circa 1800, d. after 1869 m. McMillan / m. William Turnage.

Children of William and Mary McLattan: married 1815

George Washington Turnage 1816-1875 Wilson TN
Gardner Turnage – 1818-
Sandy M. Turnage – 1819 NC to

Walker C. Turnage – 1820 Williamson Co, TN - 1875

Children of William and Lavinia Thompson married 1827

Eliza Turnage b. 1830 –1910 (Chesterfield, SC) married William Alfred Rivers
William Henry Turnage b. 8 Jun 1832, d. 28 Dec 1883 in Darlington, SC
Thomas Franklin Turnage b. 28 Aug 1834 to 1889 in Arkansas
Peter Alonzo Turnage b. 2 Aug 1839, d. 21 Jun 1911 in Marlboro, SC
Dillard Oscar Turnage+ b. 12 Feb 1837, d. bt 1877 - 1880 in Prarie, AK
\ married Sarah Jane Lampley.

GENERATION EIGHT
William G. Turnage and Mary _____

Born 1747 in Pitt, NC. Died in 1823 in Chesterfield, SC. Had 7 wives.
Parents are Luke Turnage and Rachel. Served in the American
Revolution.   Also had a wife named Mary and Elizabeth

Wives :   Mary & Elizabeth

Children:
John – 1784 in SC
William – 1774 in Pitt, NC to 1850 Chesterfield, SC (mother Mary)
Elisah – 1770-1774 approx birth
Luke – 1770-1780 approx. birth
Susan 1790 SC
Henry Michael – 1785 Chesterfield, SC and died 1873 in Tipton, TN –
        War of 1812. Married Nancy Ann Colley
Joseph Turnage – 1787-
Charity Turnage 1790-1868
Richard Turnage 1790 -

GENERATION NINE
Luke Turnage and Rachel _____?

Luke was born in 1731 Bertie, NC and died in 1818 Chesterfield, SC. His parents are William George Turnage and Selah Needham.

Children of Luke and Rachel:

Charity
William (1747 in Pitt Co NC to 1823 Chesterfield Co, SC)
John (1755 in NC to 1820 KY)

GENERATION TEN

William George Turnage and Sarah (Selah) Needham

William George TURNAGE, b 1700-1712 Bertie Co., North Carolina, d 1736 in Bertie Co., North Carolina. His parents were George and Elizabeth White Turnage.
married Sarah NEEDHAM 1730 in North Carolina, and had children: Sarah Needham was born 1705 in VA / NC area. Siblings of William George were Charity and John.

Children:

Luke TURNAGE – born 1731 in Bertie Co, NC
William George TURNAGE – 1730-1740 and died 1795 in Greene County, NC
James Turnage

GENERATION ELEVEN
George Turnage and Elizabeth White

George TURNAGE, b 7 Apr 1671, Great Waltham, Essex, England, d in Essex, England, m Elizabeth WHITE. Had child William George. He moved from Essex to NC. He is first in Chowan Co, NC (tax list) of 1717. He witnessed a deed in Bertie co., NC in 1735, sold land in Bertie Co in 1736/37 and received a Patent of land in what is now Pitt Co. NC in 1738.

He was an orphan, having lost his father when he was an infant, and his mother when he was only 3. It is still a mystery who raised George, Jr., his sister Mary and younger brother James. From old English parish records, it was discovered that George Turnage, Sr. had 2 sons named George Turnage, Jr. The first died soon after he was born. The 2nd son, born in 1671 was also named George, Jr. He was the George found on early court records in America in 1711.

George petitioned for a land grant of 200 acres about 1738 in Craven County, NC. This section of Craven County later became part of Johnston and Pitt counties. George's last name was spelled Turnedge in most of his early 1700 records.

Elizabeth White was born in 1693 and died in 1716. She married George in 1710.

George and Elizabeth White had children:

William George (1700-1770) born in Bertie County, NC
Mary Turnage
James Turnage

GENERATION TWELVE

George Turnage and Mary Ann ?

George TURNAGE, b 1647 in Great Waltham, Essex, England, d 1 Jun 1672, m Mary Ann
George and Mary Ann

Their children:

George TURNAGE

A POEM BY IVIE TURNAGE

THE OLD HOME PLACE

I went back to the home place
After many years away,
To find it all deserted
Where children used to play.

The window panes were broken
The floor had fallen in,
There were no glowing embers
Where the fireplace once had been.

No ticking on the mantle piece
Of the old clock once so dear.
Nor could I hear the creaking of
My father's favorite chair.

The kitchen seemed so quiet
No sound of mother there,
Or could I smell the fragrance
Of baking in the air.

The garden fence had fallen
The gate swung in the breeze,
There was nothing left to find
Where the sagebrush used to be.

I rushed out the orchard
To see the apple trees
To smell the lovely blossoms
And see the honey bees.

I stood there in amazement

To see it all so bare,
What many years and nature
Can do when no one cares.

By: Ivie Turnage Fletcher 1953

www.ingramcontent.com/pod-product-compliance
Lightning Source LLC
Chambersburg PA
CBHW081813280526
45789CB00008B/3114